KATHY and DAVID BLACK

SOLO TIME FOR VIOLIN

BOOK 3

Contents

With thanks to Simon Stace for reviewing the pieces in this book, Ros Stephen for recording the violin tracks, Ken Blair for producing the CD, and Laura Jones and Phil Croydon at OUP for all their help. KB & DB.

The CD includes piano-only backings for all pieces. CD credits: David Blackwell (piano).
Audio tracks for a selection of full performances are available from the catalogue page of the OUP website.

OXFORD
UNIVERSITY PRESS

Great Clarendon Street, Oxford OX2 6DP, England.
This collection and each individual work within it © Oxford University Press 2015.

Impression: 7
ISBN 978-0-19-340490-8
Music and text origination by Julia Bovee
Printed in Great Britain

1. Sinfonia in D

BWV 789

5/10

Johann Sebastian Bach (1685–1750)

arr. KB & DB

Allegro ♩ = 70

Bach is considered to be one of the greatest composers of the Baroque era, with a vast array of compositions spanning orchestral, choral, and instrumental music. His mastery of counterpoint, the interweaving of different and independent musical lines to create a unified whole, is unsurpassed in music. This piece, originally for keyboard, is an example of a three-part contrapuntal texture, a texture which Bach also used in his sonatas for violin and keyboard. All dynamics and phrase marks are editorial, and mordents should begin on the upper note.

2. Allegro

from Divertimento No. 3, K439b

Wolfgang Amadeus Mozart (1756–91)

arr. KB & DB

This movement is from a set of pieces for three basset-horns (a type of clarinet invented around 1770 and popular with composers until around 1830), believed to have been written by Mozart in the mid-1780s. The original manuscript is lost, but the pieces were published as both wind trios and in an arrangement for piano with violin (called the *Viennese Sonatinas*) in the 1800s. The structure of this piece is sonata form, a form widely used in the Classical period. The first section (the exposition) states the main themes in first the tonic and then the dominant key (here G major and D major), cadencing on the dominant at the double bar. This is followed by the development section which uses the material in different keys, before the return of the main themes in the final recapitulation section, this time in the tonic key throughout.

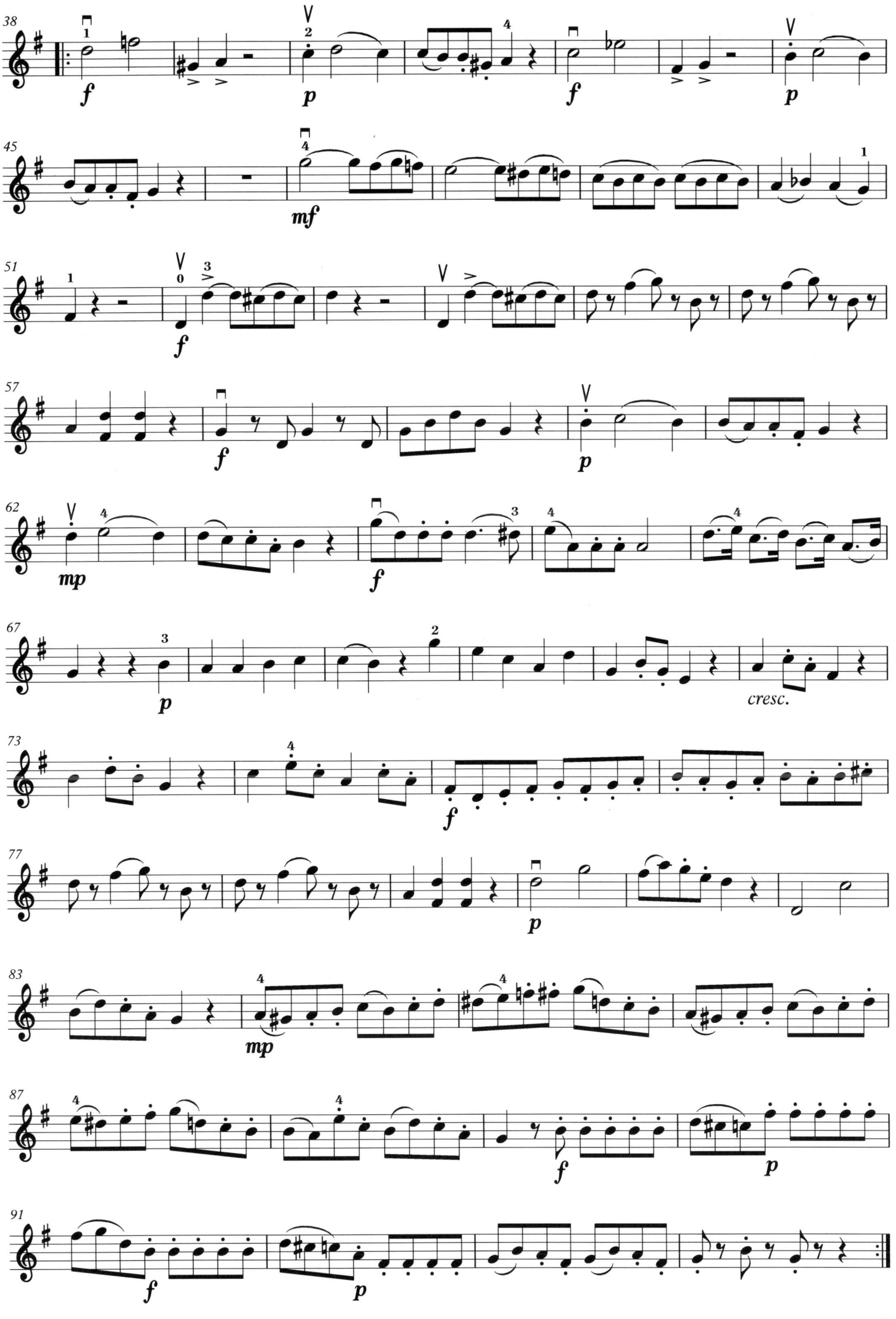
cresc.

3. Fantasia

Georg Philipp Telemann (1681–1767)
ed. KB & DB

Telemann was a prolific German Baroque composer and friend of J. S. Bach. Originally written for keyboard, this Fantasia is in ritornello form, in which the opening melody, or ritornello, recurs at points throughout the piece, separated by short sections in other keys. The version of the theme at bar/measure 40 is a suggestion only, and shows how it might be decorated in performance (players may like to invent their own decorated version). Although the time signature is **C**, the piece has the feel of $\frac{2}{2}$, much like a Baroque Gavotte with phrases beginning and ending at the half bar. All dynamics and phrase marks are editorial.

optional decorated version of ritornello theme

4. Cripple Creek

track 4

American trad.
arr. KB & DB

Traditional American fiddle music is a rich mix of different styles and influences drawn from Scottish and Irish fiddle music, jazz, and bluegrass. Bluegrass fiddle style originated in Kentucky, known as the Bluegrass state, and is characterized by a strong rhythmic drive, a virtuosic style, and 'blues notes'—notes that are 'bent' or altered for expressive effect, e.g. the flattened 3rd. This arrangement exploits some typical techniques used by traditional players: elaboration of the melody, double-stopping, left-hand pizzicato, bowing across the beat (bars 61–8), and a written-out improvised solo with inflected blues notes (C♮, bar 63). Play with energy and short, decisive bowing.

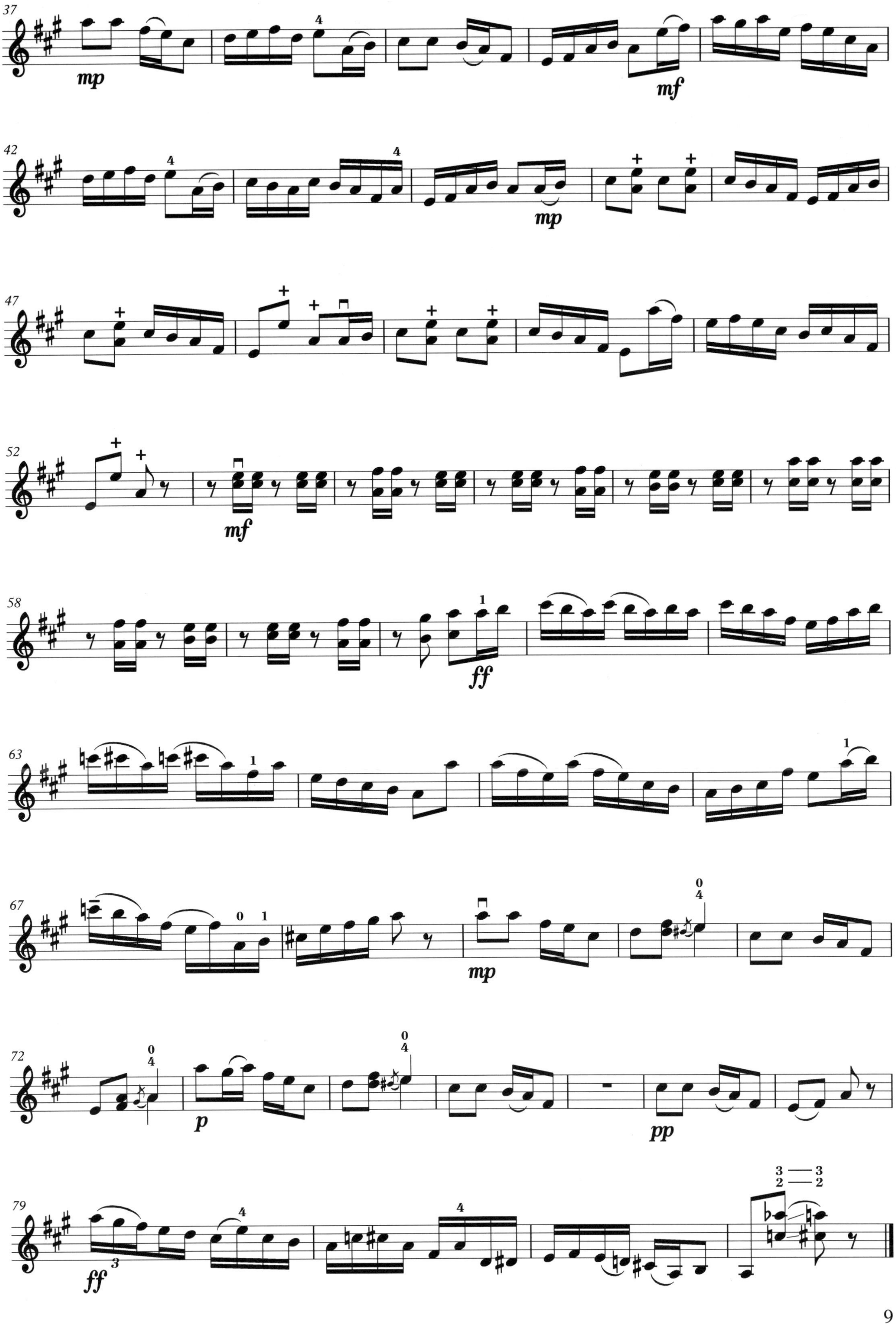
37
mp
mf
42
mp
47
52
mf
58
ff
63
67
mp
72
p
pp
79
ff

5. Mallorca

Isaac Albéniz (1860–1909)

arr. KB & DB

Andantino ♪ = 108

Albéniz was a Spanish composer and virtuoso pianist, who began a performing career at the age of nine and gave many concerts worldwide. His musical language evokes the traditional music of his native Spain with brilliant instrumental effects that suggest Flamenco guitars and Moorish inflections in the melodies, as seen here in the G♯–F♮ in bar 8. This piece is an arrangement of his piano composition, Op. 202, named after the Spanish Balearic island in the Mediterranean.

poco più mosso ♪ = 116
mp cantando dolce
poco rit. a tempo
dim.
mp
molto rit.
cresc.
f
p
a tempo
mp cantando dolce
mf
mp
(ext.)
rit.
p
a tempo
mp
poco rit. a tempo
mp
p
rit.
D.C. al Coda
dim.
CODA
p
pp

6. Puck

from *Lyric Pieces,* Op. 71 No. 3

Edvard Grieg (1843–1907)
arr. KB & DB

This piece is from the last volume of Grieg's *Lyric Pieces,* a collection of 66 pieces for solo piano published in ten books. It is a character sketch for the impish sprite and mischievous prankster from Shakespeare's *A Midsummer Night's Dream,* and a sense of fantasy—with a hint of menace—runs through the piece. A well-controlled staccato in the lower half of the bow, articulated accents, and closely observed dynamics will help convey the character of this piece.

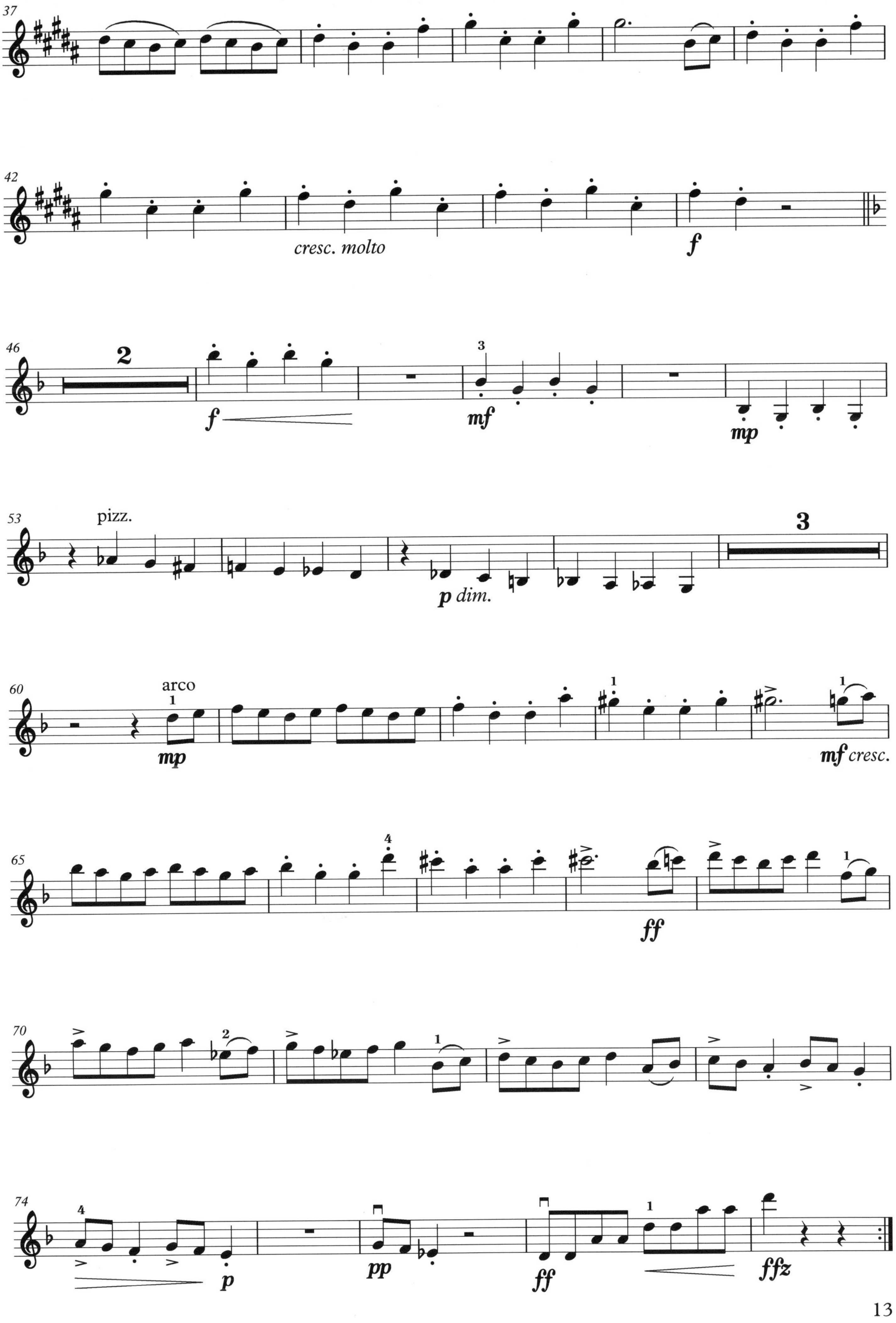
cresc. molto
pizz.
p dim.
arco
mf cresc.

for Clare

7. Jiana

Romanian trad.
arr. KB & DB

Allegro risoluto ♩ = 76

Jiana is a traditional Romanian folk dance from the villages of south Transylvania in central Romania, a mountainous region with many shepherd communities. Before World War I the Hungarian composer Béla Bartók collected folk tunes from this region and published a set for piano (later arranged for violin and piano), based on tunes originally played on fiddle or shepherd's flute; there are elements of Bartók's harmony in the short 'Lento' section of this piece. The tune uses the Dorian mode,

found in much European folk music:

Jiana should be played with a vigorous style to help capture the lively rhythms of this folk melody. The contrasting 'Lento' section is a brief, tender respite before the frantic semiquavers continue to an exciting climax.

f cresc.
(piano)
Lento ♪ = 76
p espressivo, con rubato
ten.
sul A
poco rit.
sub. tempo primo
cresc.

8. Sonatina

Edward Elgar (1857–1934)
arr. KB & DB

I. Andantino

track 8

II. Allegro

track 9

Elgar was a major English composer, well known for large-scale works, including two symphonies, The 'Enigma' Variations, concertos for violin and for cello, and *The Dream of Gerontius* for choir and orchestra. Yet he also wrote inspired miniatures, including the ever-popular *Salut d'amour* for violin and piano and this Sonatina for piano, composed in 1889 for his niece May Grafton, though not published until 1932. In the first movement the first repeat has been added to balance the second. Retaking the bow for the down bows in bars 9–13 and 33–7 will ensure even bow distribution.

dim.
cresc.
cresc.
cresc.
dim.
dim.
poco rit.
poco meno mosso ♩ = 74
p espress.
rit.
ten.
tempo primo
cresc.
allargando

9. Valse Caressante

from *Six Pieces for Violin and Piano*

Ottorino Respighi (1879–1936)
arr. KB & DB

The Italian violinist and composer Respighi is best known for his orchestral piece *Pines of Rome*. This abridged arrangement of the *Valse Caressante* ('Tender Waltz') is from *Six Pieces for Violin and Piano* (1901–6). Enjoy gliding through the shifts of position in this light-hearted salon piece.

10. Minuet

from Symphony No. 4, the 'Italian'

Felix Mendelssohn (1809–47)
arr. KB & DB

Con moto moderato ♩ = 112

A grand tour of Europe in 1829–31 took the gifted German composer Mendelssohn to Italy, where he sketched the music for what became his Symphony No. 4, the 'Italian'.

This piece is the first section, a minuet in all but name, from the third movement of that symphony.

11. Andante cantabile

from Piano Quartet, Op. 47

Robert Schumann (1810–56)

arr. KB & DB

Although Schumann wrote symphonies, concertos, and chamber music, he is best known for his piano music and songs. This piece is based on the third movement of his Piano Quartet, written (as is usual for this genre) for piano, violin, viola, and cello. The rising and falling sevenths of this lyrical and expressive melody have a yearning quality, typical of Schumann's Romantic musical language. A singing tone quality with smooth shifts and bow changes will help capture the expressive nature of this piece.

cresc.
poco mf
4 restez
poco rit. (2nd time)
a tempo
(piano)
poco rit.
a tempo
molto espress.
III restez
rit.
meno mosso ♩ = 66
pizz.
dim.

12. Surprising Variations

on a theme by Haydn

Kathy and David Blackwell

Theme

track 13

Variation 1: Bowing skills

track 14

Variation 2: Scales and arpeggios/slurs and staccato

track 15

For the note on this piece, see p. 24.

A piano-only audio track of the complete piece is available from the OUP website.

Variation 3: Double-stops

Variation 4: Minore

track 17

Variation 5: Left-hand pizzicato—Hornpipe

track 18

Finale: Grand Introduction—Ragtime—The End

The big finish:

Violinist-composers in the eighteenth and nineteenth centuries often wrote sets of variations on a theme to showcase and practise different string techniques. This set of variations, based on the theme from the slow movement of Haydn's 'Surprise' Symphony (No. 94), is a tongue-in-cheek nod to that tradition.

for Iain

13. Elite Syncopations

Scott Joplin (1867/8–1917)

arr. KB & DB

The American composer and pianist Scott Joplin is well known for his piano ragtime compositions, most notably *The Entertainer*, used in the 1973 film *The Sting*, and *Maple Leaf Rag*. This piece is typical of the style: a syncopated melody above a steady, even bassline, with the music divided into sections with regular phrases.

14. Presto

from Keyboard Suite No. 3 in D minor, HWV 428

track 21

George Frederick Handel (1685–1759)

arr. KB & DB

Handel first wrote this Presto as part of the Finale of the orchestral overture to the opera *Il pastor fido* (1712), and later adapted it as the last movement of both the Keyboard Suite No. 3 and the Organ Concerto in D minor, Op. 7 No. 4. This version is based on the keyboard suite movement, taking some details from the string writing of the opera overture. It is in the style of a violin concerto movement, with tutti sections for the full orchestra and solo episodes where the soloist would be accompanied by continuo (harpsichord and cello).

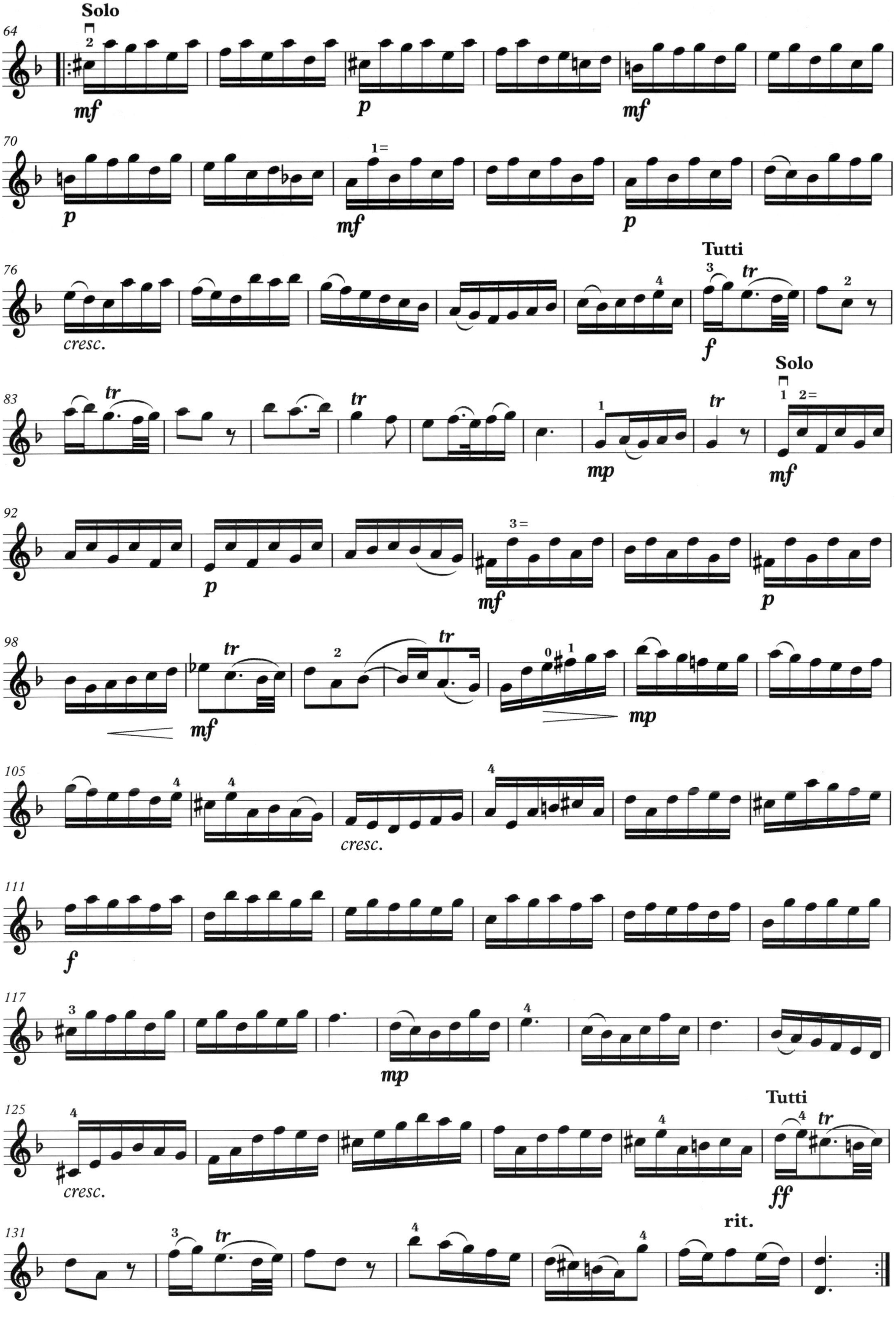
Solo
cresc.
Tutti
Solo
cresc.
cresc.
Tutti
rit.

15. Cantilène

from *Three Pieces for Organ*, Op. 29

Gabriel Pierné (1863–1937)

arr. KB & DB

A prize-winning student at the Paris Conservatoire, the French composer Gabriel Pierné was also a celebrated organist and conductor, directing amongst other works the world premiere of Stravinsky's ballet *The Firebird* in Paris in June 1910. This piece is the second of his *Three Pieces for Organ*, Op. 29. 'Cantilène' means a singing melody; aim to play the serene melody with effortless ease and with a true legato style. Keeping a steady three-beat pulse throughout the piece will help feel the rhythm of the tied notes and keep them in time.

poco rit.
a tempo
mp
p
mp
poco rit.
mf
mp
a tempo
pp
sul G
tr
mf dolcissimo
ext. 4
restez
rubato
a tempo
mp
mp
p
dim. a niente

16.   Adagio

from Violin Concerto in G, Hob. VIIa/4

Joseph Haydn (1732–1809)
ed. KB & DB

This is the second movement of Haydn's Violin Concerto in G, Hob. VIIa/4. It takes the form of a cantabile aria—a gentle, songlike melody, such as might be heard in an opera of this period, which was often richly embellished.

The dash symbol (e.g. bar 25) was used at this time to indicate staccato. The ornament realizations and the cadenza in bar 69 are suggestions.

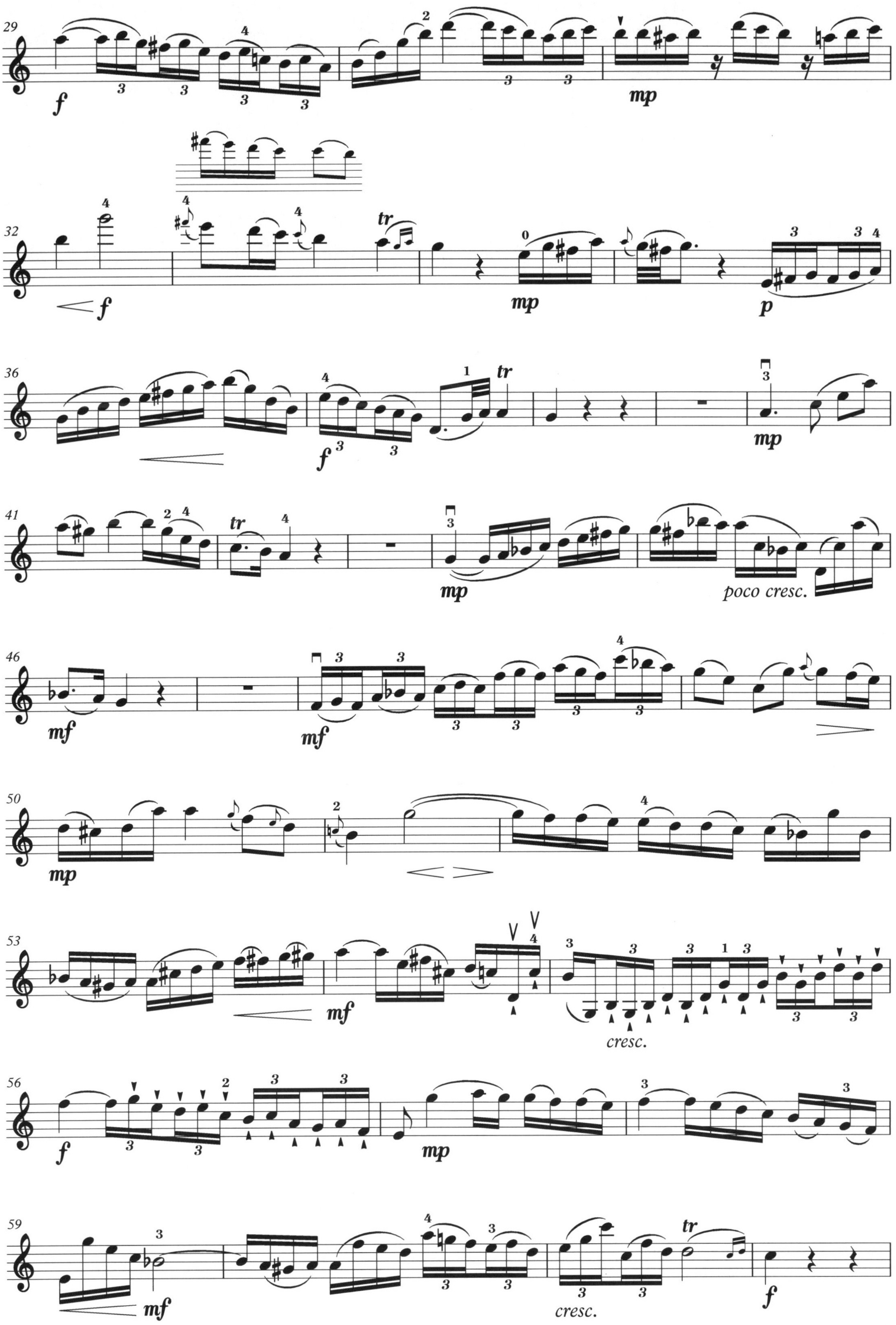
poco cresc.
cresc.
cresc.

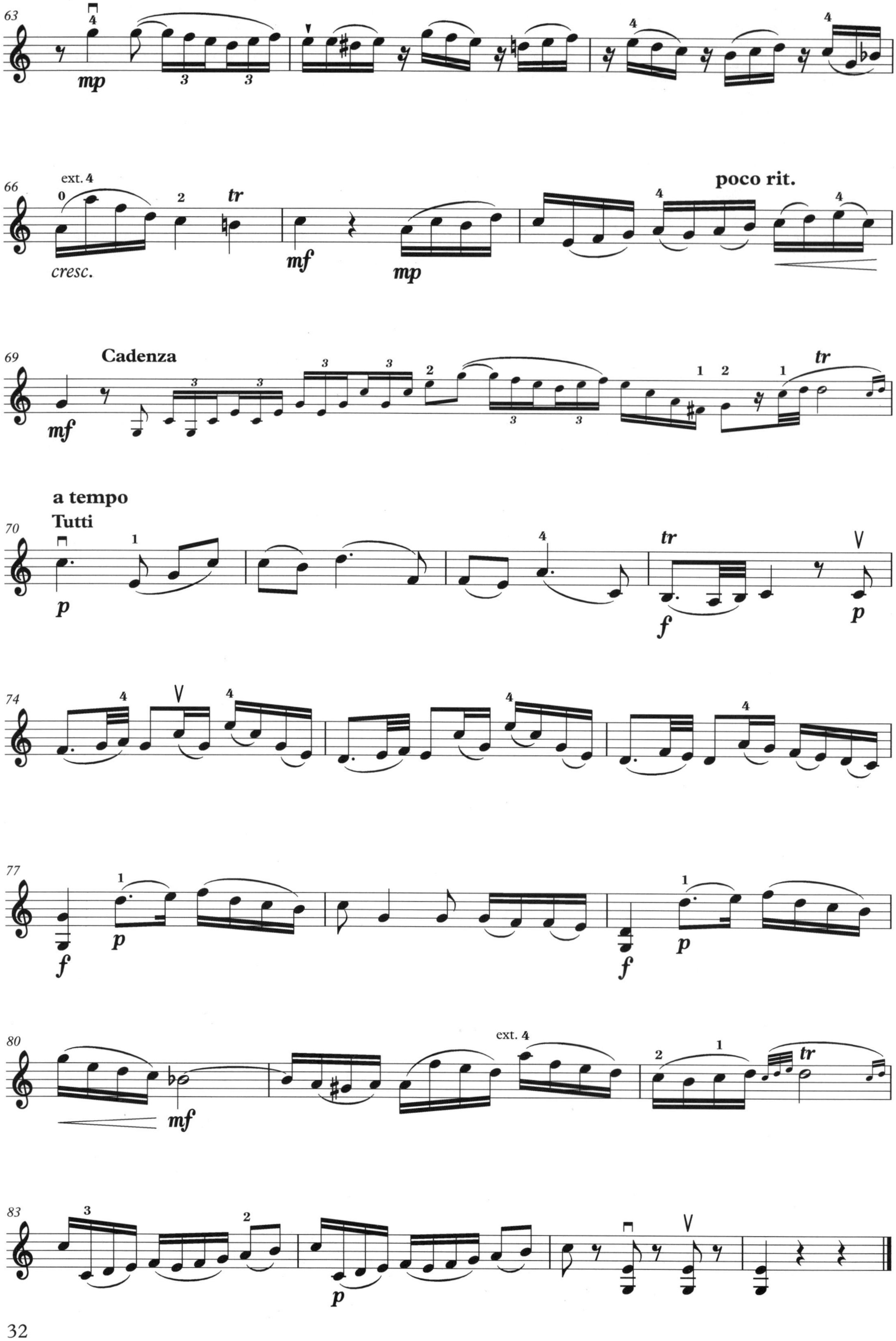
ext. 4
cresc.
poco rit.
Cadenza
a tempo
Tutti
ext. 4